Nuclear Operations

Air Force Doctrine Document 3-72
7 May 2009

Incorporating Change 2, 14 December 2011

BY ORDER OF THE
SECRETARY OF THE AIR FORCE

AIR FORCE DOCTRINE DOCUMENT 3-72
7 MAY 2009
INCORPORATING CHANGE 2, 14 December 2011 |

SUMMARY OF CHANGES

This interim change updates discussion in several places due to changes in national guidance, adds discussion of dissuasion within the overall discussion of deterrence (page 3), deletes outdated discussion of the New TRIAD (pages 5-6), and updates the organizational discussion and associated chart regarding command relationships (page 15). It also updates title numbers of referenced AFDDs throughout in accordance with a change to the Air Force doctrine publications framework.

Supersedes: AFDD 2-1.5, 15 July 1998
OPR: LeMay Center/DDS
Certified by: LeMay Center/DD (Col Todd C. Westhauser)
Pages: 41
Accessibility: Publications are available on the e-publishing website at www.e-publishing.af.mil for downloading
Releasability: There are no releasability restrictions on this publication
Approved by: Thomas K. Andersen, Major General, USAF
    Commander, Curtis E. LeMay Center for Doctrine Development and Education

FOREWORD

This doctrine provides guidance for Air Force nuclear operations. It is based on a body of knowledge gained from experience and lessons learned in organizing, training, and equipping nuclear forces in support of national security objectives. The Air Force is responsible for maintaining effective forces with the capability to support national security deterrence goals of deterring adversaries from attacking the US and its interests with their nuclear arsenals or other weapons of mass destruction (WMD); dissuading competitors from developing WMD; assuring allies and partners of the US' ability and determination to protect them; and holding at risk a specific range of targets, while placing great emphasis on the safety and security of our people and the nuclear arsenal. Achieving this in today's environment requires both an in-depth understanding of the modern world and current doctrine built on the foundation of over 60 years of experience in nuclear operations.

Credible nuclear deterrence is essential to our security and that of our allies and partners. The Air Force has no mission more sensitive than safeguarding our vital nuclear capabilities and maintaining nuclear deterrence. We must be steadfast in maintaining our nuclear expertise and the highest standards of operational discipline. Uncompromising adherence to standards, personal accountability at all levels, and leadership are the foundations upon which our success depends.

Deterrence is not limited to the threat of attack against the US. The proliferation of weapons of mass destruction (WMD), including nuclear, biological, and chemical weapons and their associated delivery systems, threatens US forces, allies and interests around the world. According to national policy, the US affirms that, for states that possess nuclear weapons and states not in compliance with their nuclear non-proliferation obligations, there remains a discrete range of contingencies in which US nuclear weapons may still play a role in deterring a conventional, chemical, or biological attack against the US or our allies and partners.

As with all doctrine, this doctrine document is authoritative, not directive. In order to more fully represent the responsibilities of those commanding and handling nuclear weapons, it contains some directive policy statements that would not normally appear in a doctrine document. This document provides a means to capture enduring deterrent principles and ensures commanders have the best guidance available to drive excellence in their day-to-day nuclear related activities.

NORTON A. SCHWARTZ
General, USAF
Chief of Staff

TABLE OF CONTENTS

INTRODUCTION

PURPOSE

This publication provides doctrinal guidance for the planning, organizing, and employment of Air Force nuclear forces. The Air Force role in nuclear operations is to organize, train, equip, and sustain forces with the capability to support the national security goals of deterring adversaries from attacking the US and its interests with their nuclear arsenals or other weapons of mass destruction; dissuading competitors from developing WMD; assuring allies and partners of the US' ability and determination to protect them; and holding at risk a specific range of targets. The fundamental purpose of the US nuclear arsenal is to deter an enemy's use of its nuclear arsenal or other weapons of mass destruction.

The threat of global nuclear war has become remote, but the risk of nuclear attack has increased. Maintaining strategic stability will be an important challenge in the years ahead. Russia and China continue to modernize their nuclear capabilities, and both claim US missile defense and conventionally-armed missile programs are destabilizing. The most immediate and extreme threat today is nuclear terrorism. The US should assume that violent extremist organizations that seek nuclear weapons would use them. Additional countries – especially those at odds with the US and its allies and partners, and the broader international community – may acquire nuclear weapons.

Much as the Cold War ended quickly, new threats could appear without warning. New governments could conceivably change the course of a country's development in such a fashion as to lead to another cold war. Tensions between the US, other countries, or rogue entities could increase to the point where a new or different deterrent strategy is required. Other strategic threats, not even imagined today, could develop in the years to come. The US cannot afford to ignore its nuclear doctrine, allowing it to sit on the shelf until another threat arises; effective strategic deterrence requires current doctrine.

Nuclear deterrence is not limited to preventing nuclear attack against the US and its allies. The development of weapons of mass destruction (WMD), including chemical, biological, radiological, and nuclear weapons and their associated delivery systems, threatens US forces, allies, partners, and interests around the world.

APPLICATION

This AFDD applies all Airmen. Unless specifically stated otherwise, Air Force doctrine applies to the full range of operations.

Doctrine is authoritative, not directive. Therefore, commanders need to consider the contents of this AFDD and the particular situation when accomplishing their missions. This document is intended neither to advocate the use of nuclear weapons nor to suggest that the US refrain from using them. It is simply designed to provide guidance to commanders, planners, and operators so that they may better develop options for civilian policymakers and ensure that the Air Force contribution to our Nation's nuclear deterrence posture is credible, robust, safe, secure and ready.

SCOPE

Nuclear operations doctrine focuses on posturing, maintaining, exercising, and employing nuclear forces for deterrence, as well as responding in a timely fashion should deterrence fail. It applies on a global scale as well as to activities within a theater of operations.

FOUNDATIONAL DOCTRINE STATEMENTS

Foundational doctrine statements are the basic principles and beliefs contained in the AFDD.

✪ Although nuclear forces are not the only factor in the deterrence equation, our nuclear capability underpins all other elements of deterrence. The fundamental purpose of the US nuclear arsenal is to deter adversaries from attacking the US and its interests with their nuclear arsenals or other weapons of mass destruction (WMD); dissuade competitors from developing WMD; and assure allies and partners of the US' ability and determination to protect them. (Page 2)

✪ The physical employment of nuclear weapons is a form of strategic attack. (Page 4)

✪ The nature of nuclear weapons is such that their use can produce political and psychological effects well beyond their actual physical effects. (Page 4)

✪ The physical employment of nuclear weapons at any level requires explicit orders from the President. (Page 4)

✪ Units supporting the nuclear mission must be appropriately trained on the full spectrum of nuclear support to include safety, security, and handling of nuclear weapons and components. (Page 5)

✪ The law of armed conflict does not expressly prohibit the possession or use of nuclear weapons. (Page 7)

✪ The destruction wrought by nuclear weapons can be immense, or it can be tailored and limited for a particular scenario. (Page 7)

✪ Effective command and control is critical for the proper employment of nuclear weapons. (Page 11)

✪ The decision whether or not to use nuclear weapons will always be made by civilian leaders. (Page 11)

✪ The goal of the Air Force Nuclear Weapons Surety Program is to incorporate maximum nuclear surety, consistent with operational requirements, from weapon system development to retirement from the inventory. (Page 20)

✪ Adversaries and allies should be highly confident of the Air Force's ability to secure nuclear weapons from accidents, theft, loss, and accidental or unauthorized use. (Page 20)

✪ Whether working with continental US-based nuclear forces or conducting theater nuclear operations, commanders must ensure the safety, security, and reliability of their weapons and associated components. (Page 20)

✪ All individuals involved with nuclear weapons are responsible for the safety of those devices. (Page 21)

✪ Nuclear weapons and their components must not be allowed to become vulnerable to loss, theft, sabotage, damage, or unauthorized use. (Page 22)

✪ Commanders are accountable for the safety, training, security, and maintenance of nuclear weapons and delivery systems, and reliability of personnel at all times. (Page 23)

✪ The credibility of the Air Force's nuclear program is founded in the skill of its combat crews and support personnel. Realistic training, high standards for technical competence, strong analytical skills, and personal reliability are key elements that shape its force. The importance of high-quality training cannot be overstated. (Page 25)

CHAPTER ONE

FUNDAMENTALS OF NUCLEAR OPERATIONS

The United States seeks the peace and security of a world without nuclear weapons. However, as long as nuclear weapons exist, deterring nuclear attack on the United States, our allies, and partners will continue to be the fundamental role of U.S. nuclear weapons.

-- The National Military Strategy of the United States of America, 2011

The end of the Cold War has had a major impact on the perceived utility and role of nuclear weapons in the US. Force reductions have reduced the specter of a large-scale, Cold War-type nuclear exchange; however, as long as nuclear weapons exist, the possibility of their use remains. This risk is aggravated as potential adversaries seek to acquire nuclear weapons and other weapons of mass destruction (WMD). This continuing proliferation places US forces, allies, and civilians around the world at greater risk. Thus, while nuclear operations are not as visible a component of national security as they were during the Cold War, they continue to underpin US deterrence.

US nuclear policy is not static and is shaped by numerous considerations. As the civilian leadership changes US policy due to new threats or technologies, the Air Force will need to develop new concepts, systems, and procedures. For instance, the concepts of "mutual assured destruction" and "flexible response" required different types of weapons, different plans, and different degrees of survivability for command and control (C2) systems. Stated policies also affect the ability to deter an enemy. As an example, US policy on using nuclear weapons to respond to an adversary's battlefield use of WMD is purposely vague. The ambiguous nature of US policy makes it impossible for an enemy to assume such a response would not be forthcoming. Even though there is no guarantee nuclear force would be used to respond to a WMD attack, planners are responsible for making alternative options available for civilian policymakers.

This chapter examines the context of Air Force nuclear operations: its day-to-day role as an element of deterrence and in providing strategic effects; a summary of key employment considerations; weapons effects; war termination; and additional considerations.

DETERRENCE

Deterrence is fundamental to national security. Per Joint Publication (JP) 1-02, *Department of Defense Dictionary of Military and Associated Terms*, "Deterrence is the prevention from action by fear of the consequences. Deterrence is a state of mind brought about by the existence of a credible threat of unacceptable counteraction." For a nation whose security is predicated on an enduring strategy of dissuasion and deterrence, a failure of deterrence is a fundamental risk.

Although nuclear forces are not the only factor in the deterrence equation, our nuclear capability underpins all other elements of deterrence. The fundamental purpose of the US nuclear arsenal is to deter adversaries from attacking the US and its interests with their nuclear arsenals or other WMD; dissuade competitors from developing WMD; and assure allies and partners of the US' ability and determination to protect them. Additionally, our nuclear forces assure allies of our continuing commitment to their security, dissuade potential adversaries from embarking on programs or activities that could threaten our vital interests, and defeat threats that are not deterred.

Deterrence can be described as a state of mind created in an adversary's (or potential adversary's) leadership. Their leadership should believe the cost of aggression against the US, its interests, or its allies will be so high as to outweigh any possible gain. Deterrence requires the US to maintain the ability to use force, which means having trained, capable, ready, and survivable forces; a robust command, control, communications, computers, intelligence, surveillance, and reconnaissance structure; and timely, flexible, and adaptive planning capabilities. The second critical element of deterrence is the will to use nuclear weapons. If an enemy believes these tools will not be used, then their deterrent value is zero.

The cumulative effects of deterrence and assurance stem from the credibility of our nuclear capabilities in the minds of those we seek to deter, dissuade, or assure. To achieve its psychological and political objectives of deterring opponents and reassuring allies, deterrence requires visible and credible nuclear capabilities. This credibility is attained through focused day-to-day training, periodic exercises, and regular inspections which ensures precise, reliable nuclear forces that prove our capability and will to use them if the situation warrants.

Extended Deterrence

During the Cold War the US provided for the security of its allies by threatening a nuclear response in the event of an attack on them by the Soviet Union. This policy, based on the threat of retaliation, served as the foundation for what is now called extended deterrence. Extended deterrence remains an important pillar of US policy; however, its application in the context of the 21st century is very different from the Cold War. Today, extended deterrence is less about retaliation and more about posturing to convince an enemy that they are unlikely to achieve the political and military objectives behind any attack on the US or one of our allies.

Through alliances and treaties, our extended deterrence strategy provides a nuclear umbrella to friendly and allied nations. Our nuclear umbrella assures allies of our commitment to their security and serves as a nonproliferation tool by obviating their need to develop and field their own nuclear arsenals.

In the case of the North Atlantic treaty Organization (NATO), the deployment of nuclear weapons in Europe is not a Service or regional command issue—it is an Alliance issue. Moreover, actions concerning nuclear posture in NATO have an impact on the perceptions of our allies elsewhere.

Dissuasion

Through a cohesive strategy of political, economic, diplomatic and military capabilities, adversaries are discouraged from competing with US strategic nuclear forces militarily because consequences are severe and restraint is rewarded.

STRATEGIC EFFECTS

JP 1-02 defines effects as "the physical or behavioral state of a system that results from an action, a set of actions, or another effect." It is the convincing and widely recognized ability to execute and influence the perceptions, plans, and actions of one's adversaries that constitutes the essence of deterrence, which is the cornerstone of our nation's strategic effects. Our day-to-day precise, reliable nuclear operations, underpinned by the unquestionable credibility of being prepared and able to execute a nuclear strike, are the heart of US Air Force responsibility and accountability for the nuclear deterrent mission.

Deterrence and Escalation Control: The Yom Kippur War

Following a three-week assault by Egypt and Syria in 1973, Israel Defense Forces (IDF) pushed Arab forces back beyond the original lines due in large part to US resupply. The US perception of the threat of unilateral Soviet action, including a communiqué from Soviet leader Leonid Brezhnev and the alerting of Soviet airborne divisions, led President Nixon to reposition bombers and tankers and raise the nuclear and conventional alert forces posture to DEFCON 3. The US administration called Brezhnev's communiqué, which threatened unilateral action, "a matter of gravest concern" and decried its likely "incalculable consequences." In fact, President Nixon's response to the Soviets, in the form of a note drafted by Secretary of State Kissinger, posited that "Should the two great nuclear powers be called upon to provide force, it would introduce an extremely dangerous potential for great-power rivalry in the area." In the end, this language, the US DEFCON 3 posture, and Kissinger's steadfast resolve during the press conference at the State Department demonstrated the US's commitment to preserving its strategic objectives and balance of power in the Middle East. The US actions and statements proved to be successful in defusing the conflict.

-- *"Effects-Based Operations: The Yom Kippur War Case Study"*

The physical employment of nuclear weapons is a form of strategic attack. Strategic attack is "offensive action specifically selected to achieve national strategic objectives. These attacks seek to weaken the adversary's ability or will to engage in conflict, and may achieve strategic objectives without necessarily having to achieve operational objectives as a precondition" (AFDD 3-70, *Strategic Attack*). It is an offensive operation intended to accomplish national, multinational, or theater strategic-level objectives without necessarily engaging an enemy's fielded military forces. However, this does not preclude operations to destroy the enemy's fielded forces if required to accomplish strategic national objectives.

The nature of nuclear weapons is such that their use can produce political and psychological effects well beyond their actual physical effects. The employment of nuclear weapons may lead to such unintended consequences as escalation of the current conflict or long-term deterioration of relations with other countries. For this reason above all others, the decision whether or not to use, or even threaten to use, nuclear weapons will always be a political decision and not a military one, and will be made by civilian leaders. Additionally, the viability of deterrence relies on credible nuclear forces whose value resides in achieving national security goals through daily deterrent operations without the physical employment of nuclear weapons.

The physical employment of nuclear weapons at any level requires explicit orders from the President. Nuclear weapons are unique in their destructive power and psychological impact. The use of nuclear weapons represents a significant escalation from conventional warfare. The decision to employ nuclear weapons is a political decision and will only be made by

---

Does the United States Still Need Nuclear Weapons?

The world has changed a great deal in the last decade and a half. The Cold War stand-off with the Soviet Union is over, and Russia is no longer an ideological adversary. The United States has made historic reductions in its operationally deployed strategic nuclear forces and plans to reduce them to a level of 1,700 to 2,200 by 2012, as called for by the Moscow Treaty. The U.S. has also greatly reduced its non-strategic nuclear forces and the total nuclear warhead stockpile. These significant nuclear reductions are fully warranted in the new security environment.

The United States continues to maintain nuclear forces for two fundamental reasons. First, the international security environment remains dangerous and unpredictable, and has grown more complicated since the dissolution of the Soviet Union. Political intentions can change overnight and technical surprises can be expected. Second, nuclear weapons continue to play unique roles in supporting U.S. national security. Although not suited for every 21st century challenge, nuclear weapons remain an essential element in modern strategy.

-- DOE/DOD White Paper, "National Security and Nuclear Weapons in the 21st Century," September 2008

national leadership to support national objectives. In the US, the President retains sole authority for the execution and termination of nuclear operations.

NUCLEAR OPERATIONS IN SUPPORT OF THEATER OBJECTIVES

The US employs extended deterrence on a daily basis to project deterrent effects in key regions across the globe. These forward-deployed assets combined with the global reach of continental United States (CONUS)-based nuclear forces provide theater-level assurance to allies abroad and deterrence to adversaries. Should deterrence fail, Air Force forces operating in a theater environment may be called upon to use nuclear weapons in order to obtain theater-level objectives. Though often referred to as "tactical" weapons, the designation is misleading. Terming the effect "tactical" implies attaining only limited military objectives. Activities at the tactical level of war focus on the arrangement and maneuver of combat elements in relation to each other and the enemy. While the use of nuclear weapons will affect an ongoing engagement between friendly and enemy forces, their use should also be designed to help achieve the political goals of the operation. Such use will additionally have an impact on the US's long-term relations with other countries.

In order to achieve theater-level objectives, combatant commanders (CCDRs) may request the use of CONUS-based intercontinental ballistic missiles (ICBMs) or theater-level nuclear weapons using either long-range bombers or fighters designated as "dual-capable;" i.e., capable of both nuclear and conventional operations. Cruise missiles allow for standoff attack which puts crew members at minimal risk and may deny an adversary significant tactical warning. Gravity bombs allow more flexibility in employment but put crew members at direct risk in a high-threat environment. Their delivery platforms, whether bombers or fighter aircraft, may require significant support in the form of aerial refueling or electronic warfare escort.

Units supporting the nuclear mission must be appropriately trained on the full spectrum of nuclear support to include safety, security, and handling of nuclear weapons and components. Generation to cover a nuclear tasking is a significant paradigm shift for those operating and supporting these forces; nuclear generation also removes assets from conventional tasking. Due to the operational tempo of such forces, training should be carefully balanced between the competing conventional and nuclear demands. Readiness and training requirements for Air Force nuclear forces in support of geographic combatant commands are determined by the respective CCDR with advice from the Air Force component commander.

Since the US is unlikely to engage in a major conflict unilaterally, the use of theater-level nuclear weapons would presumably occur while working in conjunction with other nations' militaries. When operating with members of treaty organizations, standardized nuclear policies may already exist. When functioning as part of a short-term coalition, however, common procedures for coalition forces should be developed during that conflict.

NUCLEAR FORCE STRUCTURE

The US nuclear force structure consists of ICBMs, bombers and dual-capable aircraft, and submarine-launched ballistic missiles (SLBMs). Each nuclear-capable asset offers distinct advantages. SLBMs are the most survivable. ICBMs offer a prompt, on-alert response capability plus dispersed fielding and numbers that deter attack. Bombers and dual- capable aircraft offer unique mission flexibility and distinct signaling in crisis. This variety of nuclear forces provides a deterrence posture suitable for the contemporary environment, credible to adversaries and reassuring to allies.

US nuclear C2 systems and effective capabilities for real-time intelligence and warning, in concert with active and passive defenses, secure and reinforce the credibility of US nuclear forces.

Additionally, the US nuclear stockpile enabling this force structure is supported by a physical infrastructure comprised of the national security laboratories and a complex of supporting facilities and equipment where modernization efforts remain essential. Equally imperative is the responsibility to maintain a highly capable workforce with the specialized skills needed to sustain the nuclear enterprise. A modern infrastructure coupled with expert human capital enhances nuclear credibility and fortifies strategic deterrence at its foundation.

In summary, as long as nuclear weapons exist, the US will maintain safe, secure, and effective nuclear forces, including deployed and stockpiled nuclear weapons, highly capable nuclear delivery systems and C2 capabilities, and the physical infrastructure and expert personnel needed to sustain them.

EMPLOYMENT

Different targeting strategies can enhance deterrent capability and, if employed, successfully achieve warfighting objectives. Changing circumstances will also affect the conditions under which the US should be prepared to employ nuclear weapons. An understanding of these issues is critical for the nuclear planner or commander at the global or theater level of conflict.

Targeting

Understanding the current strategic environment is essential to the development of a comprehensive nuclear employment strategy. Whether the enemy consists of a nation-state, rogue state, or is a non-state actor helps define the nature of the strategy. Regardless, deterrence, the ability to discourage enemy attack, is still a foundational concept in nuclear operations. Understanding the nature of deterrence, including the requirements to act if it fails, helps commanders and planners develop effective targeting strategies for nuclear employment.

As stated in AFDD 3-60, *Targeting*, "Targeting is a central component of Air Force operational art." A targeting strategy allows commanders and planners to choose the best ways to attain desired outcomes by melding ends (objectives and end states), ways (actions and effects of actions leading to the ends), and risk (the probable "cost" of attaining the ends in terms of lives, equipment, effort, time, and opportunities). Since joint and Air Force targeting doctrine encompasses both kinetic and non-kinetic employment to achieve desired effects, a complete nuclear targeting strategy must include a thorough understanding of the role of deterrence.

In order to accomplish objectives using non-kinetic means, deterrence focuses on preventing an actual exchange through demonstrating the commitment to employ weapons when required. The deterrence effort should be a clearly visible part of the strategy employed on a continuous basis through all instruments of national power. Examples include clear diplomatic and informational efforts including declaratory statements involving US nuclear posture and the commitment to act when required, military preparedness demonstrated through exercises and daily training, and economic incentives toward non proliferation efforts.

If a nuclear option is chosen, ending a conflict as soon as possible and on terms favorable to the US and/or its allies will help determine the level and scope of employment. Limiting unintended or collateral effects, consistent with AFDD 3-60 and JP 3-60, *Joint Targeting*, can help minimize and mitigate enemy reactions such that they pursue a quick cessation of hostilities as well. Careful consideration should be given to containing effects to the maximum extent possible. Although there will undoubtedly be longer-term effects from nuclear employment, commanders and planners should develop consequence management into their strategies and remain consistent with law of armed conflict principles.

Law of Armed Conflict

The "law of armed conflict" is not based on a single treaty but is instead grounded in various treaties, customs, and national practices regarding the conduct of armed conflict. This body of international law protects combatants and noncombatants, safeguards human rights, and facilitates the achievement of peace by limiting the amount of force and the manner in which it can be applied. While there is a connection between the destruction of life and property and the defeat of enemy armed forces, neither the law of armed conflict nor US policy sanction devastation as an end unto itself. That having been said, **the law of armed conflict does not expressly prohibit the possession or use of nuclear weapons**. Under international law, the use of a nuclear weapon is based on the same targeting rules applicable to the use of any other lawful weapon, i.e., the counterbalancing principles of military necessity, proportionality, distinction, and unnecessary suffering.

WEAPON EFFECTS

The destruction wrought by nuclear weapons can be immense, or it can be tailored and limited for a particular scenario. The physical impact of a nuclear strike includes both short- and long-term effects. Beyond the physical repercussions are significant psychological and political effects, which may lead to unintended consequences.

The physical effects of nuclear weapons are pronounced. The degree of destruction depends upon a number of factors such as weapon design and yield, location and height of burst, weather, and others. Planners must consider the political and military objectives and the desired degree of destruction as well as the local conditions, available weapons, and delivery systems. The immediate operational impact of a nuclear detonation varies and may come from blast and heat, the subsequent electromagnetic pulse (EMP), or more far-reaching effects, depending on the variables discussed above. This will have an immediate effect on enemy forces, logistics, and C2. Communications and computer capability will be severely

The decision to employ nuclear weapons carries significant political and psychological implications.

impacted by EMP, which is an operational effect that may lead to a long-term, strategic impact if the enemy is unable to completely restore those capabilities. Another operational effect with strategic implications is radiation, which will limit the effectiveness of enemy forces as they take protective measures but may also render enemy territory uninhabitable for a long period of time. Other significant effects may include extreme overpressure, dust, and debris.

Theater commanders and planners must consider that the operating environment after a nuclear exchange can be equally inhospitable for friendly forces. Movement through an area that has experienced a nuclear detonation will be slow because significant protective measures are required. Nuclear hardened communications and information systems are designed to be survivable in a nuclear environment and are expected to be available. The use of nuclear weapons to repel enemy forces in friendly territory will lead to long-term effects that may be unacceptable.

There are psychological effects associated with nuclear weapons that go beyond physical destruction. Notwithstanding the stark difference in physical effects between nuclear and conventional weapons, the use of nuclear weapons will have additional implications. It is difficult to determine exactly what that effect might be. A limited use of nuclear weapons may convince an enemy that the US is committed to using whatever degree of force is required and encourage them to cease and desist. It may have the opposite effect, enraging the enemy to the point where it escalates the conflict. When planning a nuclear option, it is important to consider the potential psychological impact as well as the enemy's ability to escalate.

Nuclear weapon use may also have short- and long-term negative effects on relations with other countries. The use of such weapons may be unacceptable to allies or other friendly nations. Their support for the conflict may be lost, and long-term relations may be damaged. It also has the potential to spur other nations to develop nuclear weapons. The President will make the ultimate decision, and he or she will have to consider all of these factors. Military planners and commanders should understand these factors, too, so they can present military options in the full context of their effects rather than in isolation.

WAR TERMINATION

The goal behind using nuclear weapons is to achieve US political objectives and resolve a conflict on terms favorable to the US. Nuclear operations, like all military operations, should use the minimum force necessary and should be terminated once the objectives have been attained. This requires that decisive targets be struck first, mandating the need for effective intelligence and targeting capabilities. While nuclear operations are in progress, a reliable C2 system is essential if operations are to be terminated when no longer needed or continued if required. Finally, the US must maintain forces in reserve which will continue to protect against coercion following a nuclear strike, convincing the adversary that further hostilities on its part will be met by a swift response.

Assessment is a critical tool for understanding when to terminate and when to continue the attack. Assessment is "a continuous process that measures the overall effectiveness of employing joint force capabilities during military operations. It is also the determination of the progress toward accomplishing a task, creating an effect, or achieving an objective" (JP 1-02). Assessment supports the commander's decision making process by providing insight into the validity of the strategy and accompanying plans. In terms of nuclear operations, it is thus a critical tool for understanding whether national objectives have been achieved, as well as when to terminate and when to continue an attack.

Refer to AFDD 3-0, *Operations and Planning*, for more discussion on establishing assessment criteria.

ADDITIONAL CONSIDERATIONS

The day-to-day purpose of nuclear weapons is to deter; to create desired political effects without actually employing nuclear weapon kinetic effects. Deterrence is a political tool which can be postured to affect the desired outcome. Civilian leadership can send strong messages to assure our allies and dissuade our adversaries through strategic messaging, generation of forces, posturing the forces, deployment of forces, and limited strikes to show our resolve and/or provide escalation control.

The decision to use nuclear weapons is one made only after careful consideration of all relevant factors. One issue which should be addressed is whether the objectives may be achieved through other means, either those offered by non-nuclear, long-range strike capabilities or by other conventional capabilities. The use of nuclear weapons carries with it the potential for undesirable political consequences. There also may be additional logistical requirements associated with employing such weapons. Commanders and planners should consider exactly what effects they are trying to produce and consider non-nuclear alternatives as well.

If the focus of operations is on physical impact, other munitions may provide the degree of limited or widespread destruction desired without the long-term effects that would result from nuclear weapons. Precision-guided munitions may allow for destruction of hardened facilities without excessive collateral damage. Cluster munitions may be used to destroy or deny a wide area.

Psychological effects can also be achieved with conventional munitions, if the goal is to strike fear in an adversary's leadership or fielded forces. Operations DESERT STORM in 1991 and IRAQI FREEDOM in 2003 demonstrated that a combination of heavy aerial bombardment and military information support operations can severely degrade an enemy's operational effectiveness.

Planners should fully understand the political and military objectives before advocating the use of nuclear weapons. Depending upon the goal of the attack, it may be possible and preferable to use conventional weapons to achieve the desired effects.

SUMMARY

The Air Force's role in nuclear deterrence is to provide secure, safe, reliable and ready forces in support of our national nuclear deterrent capability. Deterrence forces can be tailored to fit particular threats and respond to a broad array of challenges to domestic and international security. The role of nuclear weapons is to deter adversaries from attacking the US and its interests with their nuclear arsenals or other WMD; dissuade competitors from developing WMD; assure allies and partners of the US' ability and determination to protect them; and, should deterrence fail, to terminate the conflict as quickly as possible on terms favorable to the US.

Commanders must be prepared to provide nuclear options to the President and Secretary of Defense (SecDef). If the US is to engage in nuclear operations, planners should have a clear understanding of the objectives involved, the conditions in the theater, the disposition of forces, and the weapons available. Commanders should attempt to terminate hostilities as quickly as possible but should be prepared to continue operations as needed. Nuclear operations involve issues beyond simply launching weapons, and commanders should understand the constraints that will be placed upon their employment.

CHAPTER TWO

COMMAND AND CONTROL OF NUCLEAR OPERATIONS

The United States command and control system has provided a high degree of control through the history of the United States nuclear weapons program. Perhaps one of the biggest dangers faced from new nuclear powers is a lack of a sophisticated system to control their nuclear weapons.

— Richard A. Paulsen,
The Role of US Nuclear Weapons in the Post-Cold War Era

Effective C2 is critical for the proper employment of nuclear weapons. C2 is defined as "the exercise of authority and direction by a properly designated commander over assigned and attached forces in the accomplishment of the mission" (JP 1-02). A strong C2 capability allows for employment of the proper force against a target in a timely manner. It also provides the means to order the termination of a conflict and avoid further escalation. C2 is a vital component of US deterrent capability, as it guarantees the ability of the US to respond even after suffering an attack. C2 systems should be designed to operate vertically and horizontally to allow effective control of nuclear assets and forces by the President at all affected levels. Proper planning and implementation will ensure that C2 systems are interoperable, secure, timely, efficient, and survivable. Nuclear C2 is a vital aspect of our nuclear deterrent capability. Visible worldwide exercises must routinely highlight capabilities to our allies and adversaries.

AUTHORIZATION FOR USE OF NUCLEAR WEAPONS

The decision whether or not to use nuclear weapons will always be made by civilian leaders. The President of the United States is the only person with the authority to order their use. Working with the SecDef, the President may determine nuclear weapons are required to resolve a situation. The President will issue the execution order through the Chairman of the Joint Chiefs of Staff (CJCS) to the CCDR and, ultimately, to the forces in the field exercising direct control over the weapons.

To allow for the timely execution of this order, a series of emergency action procedures (EAP) allow for a quick response to an authentic execution message. EAP should be simple enough to allow for rapid action while at the same time ensuring that an execution order is valid and authentic. Personnel involved in the actual employment of nuclear weapons must be intensively trained and certified in these procedures so they can respond quickly while at the same time resolving any problems that might occur in the transmission of the order.

Positive Release Orders

To prevent unauthorized employment of nuclear weapons, certain code systems are used to validate the authenticity of nuclear orders. Access to these systems and codes are tightly controlled to ensure unauthorized individuals are not permitted to gain access to the means to order or terminate nuclear weapons employment. Conversely, once appropriate orders have been sent, weapon system operators must respond in a timely manner if weapons are to be employed effectively before the situation changes. This requires a standard set of procedures for initiating or terminating operations. Knowledge of these procedures could allow an adversary to determine the time required to conduct operations and the methods crew members will use to accomplish them, allowing that adversary to take more effective measures to counter or limit a nuclear strike. Though CONUS-based nuclear weapon systems have an information security structure in place, theater commanders need to consider how best to protect information in a forward-deployed location. They may turn to supporting commands and agencies for assistance, such as United States Strategic Command (USSTRATCOM), the National Security Agency, and the Air Force Office of Special Investigations. Allowing unauthorized persons to have knowledge of nuclear procedures can sharply reduce operational effectiveness. As with all components of force protection, information security and operations security are critical to mission success.

COMMUNICATION SYSTEMS

The nuclear environment can seriously degrade the ability of the civilian leadership to communicate with forces in the field. If nuclear weapons have already been employed by the US or an adversary, an EMP may have damaged communication systems, command centers may have been destroyed, and essential links may no longer be effective. The means must exist to exercise positive control over nuclear forces. Therefore, C2 systems supporting nuclear operations should be survivable, redundant, secure, and interoperable.

Survivability

C2 links should be able to survive in a chemical, biological, radiological, or nuclear (CBRN) environment. A conventional conflict can also interfere with US ability to exercise control over dispersed forces. While some systems are "soft" by their nature, and will probably not be usable after an initial exchange of weapons, other systems must be able to survive. Airborne or mobile command posts and space-based communication links can allow C2 elements to be removed from the direct conflict. Certain types of radio systems will be able to operate in a degraded environment and must be made available for nuclear C2.

Redundancy

The effects of nuclear weapons on communications will vary by system. To ensure communications are available, redundant systems are in place in the event one or more lose their effectiveness. Use of redundant systems also enhances deterrence by denying an enemy the opportunity to destroy friendly C2 capability with a single blow.

Secure Versus Nonsecure Communications Systems

Secure communications systems afford friendly forces the ability to issue orders while denying valuable intelligence to an enemy. They can also help ensure messages passed to nuclear forces are authentic and not part of enemy deception operations. However, encryption systems by their nature may garble messages or slow their transmission rates, the possibility of which may not be acceptable. The use of code systems with nonsecure communications may be more appropriate than encryption and decryption, though they do not have all of the same capabilities. C2 personnel should strike the appropriate balance between security, timeliness, and accuracy, depending on the contingency and the enemy intelligence threat.

Interoperability

C2 communications systems need to be interoperable so critical information can be exchanged following a nuclear attack. Communications systems that use proprietary information technology standards are closed systems, and their value will be severely limited if they do not interoperate with other proprietary systems. At a minimum, these systems should employ information technology standards from the Joint Technical Architecture.

INTELLIGENCE, SURVEILLANCE, AND RECONNAISSANCE

Robust intelligence, surveillance, and reconnaissance (ISR) assets are critical to planning, conducting, and assessing nuclear operations. ISR assets provide commanders with the ability to gather information and make timely decisions while supplying planners with information needed to identify decisive targets and determine weapons selection. Additionally, multiple source ISR assets enable civilian leaders with the ability to send timely and targeted deterrent signals to our adversaries and assurance to our allies as well as providing essential post-strike assessment of both friendly and enemy situations to determine follow-on operations.

Space assets provide essential information for early warning and attack assessment, as well as enemy strike or nuclear detonation detection. Airborne assets are also critical for target detection and damage assessment. Nuclear planners and commanders should have easy access to the information gathered from appropriate ISR sources.

AIR FORCE ORGANIZATION FOR CONUS-BASED NUCLEAR OPERATIONS

The Air Force is responsible for organizing, training, and equipping ICBM, bomber, reconnaissance, and air refueling forces for nuclear combat operations. Air Force major commands (MAJCOMs) and numbered Air Forces oversee the day-to-day operations of these forces. The Air Force contribution to nuclear operations includes ICBMs, nuclear-capable bombers and fighters, tankers, and reconnaissance and surveillance aircraft. Today, except for ICBMs, these forces have conventional missions in addition to their nuclear role.

Rather than organizing with individual Service components, nuclear forces within USSTRATCOM, when generated, are organized by functional task forces. For example, Task Force 214 consists of ICBMs; Task Force 204 includes nuclear-capable bombers and airborne reconnaissance; and Task Force 294 includes air refueling aircraft and airlift support. See figure 2-1. Comparable task forces exist for the Navy's submarines and for airborne communications. Each task force may have its own commander. Within each task force, forces are arrayed internally into wings, groups, and squadrons as necessary to provide internal span of control. When forces are engaged in nuclear operations, the Commander, USSTRATCOM exercises operational control (OPCON) of assigned and attached nuclear forces and delegates tactical control (TACON) to the task force commanders for mission accomplishment. It is important to note that the task force commanders are not joint commanders within the normal constellation of joint force commanders. The task force commanders also have administrative control (ADCON) responsibilities for organizing, training, and equipping

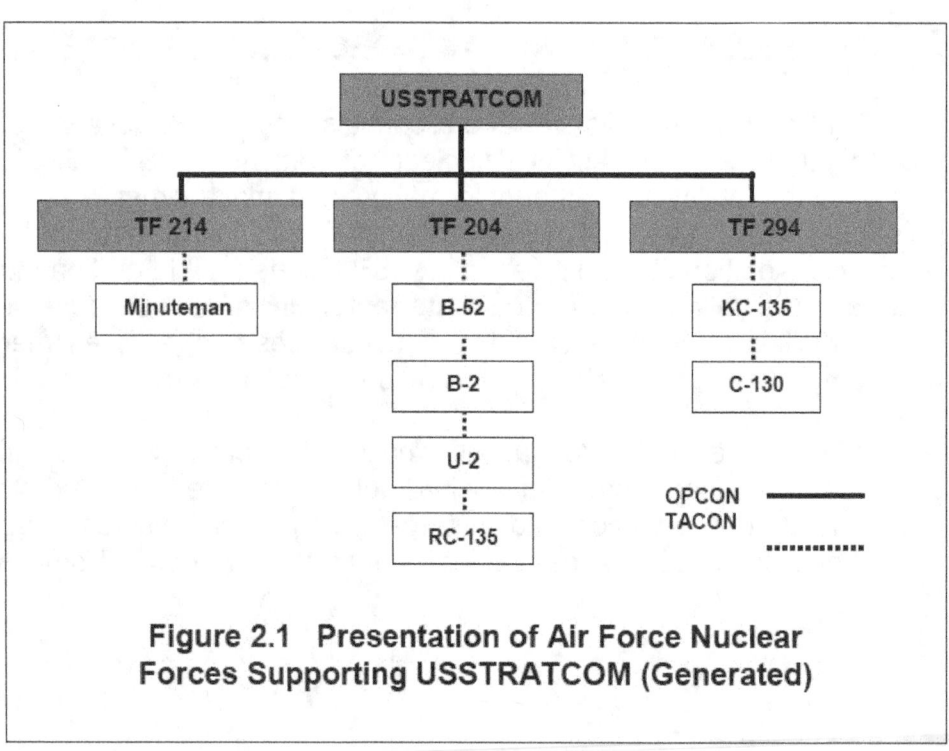

Figure 2.1   Presentation of Air Force Nuclear Forces Supporting USSTRATCOM (Generated)

14

through their owning MAJCOMs. The roles and responsibilities of the senior Air Force commanders should be clearly delineated in writing.

This structure deviates from standard Air Force organizational doctrine. Under normal conditions Air Force units assigned or attached to a joint force commander at any level should be organized along the lines of an air expeditionary task force and commanded by a single Commander, Air Force Forces (COMAFFOR). This individual would typically exercise OPCON and specified ADCON over the assigned and attached Air Force forces. However, there is not normally a COMAFFOR or joint force air component commander in the USSTRATCOM nuclear command structure. This unique organizational structure is due to the political and military aspects of nuclear force daily alert posture and the highly centralized C2 requirements of a nuclear strike.

AIR FORCE ORGANIZATION FOR THEATER-BASED NUCLEAR OPERATIONS

Geographic CCDRs may be tasked to develop and execute nuclear operations in their areas of responsibility using their assigned and attached forces. When so postured, the process for C2 of Air Force theater nuclear forces should be similar to that of CONUS-based forces:

✪ Theater nuclear forces are under the operational control of the CCDR.

✪ Nuclear execution and termination authority rests with the President.

Nuclear C2 requires implementation of stringent EAP to ensure positive authentication, validation, and release of nuclear weapons. The levels of security and integrity in these procedures are no less than for CONUS-based nuclear forces.

As with CONUS-based nuclear forces, Air Force Service component commanders in theaters have no part in nuclear execution; execution authority remains vested with national leadership. Most importantly, Air Force commanders at all levels (e.g., wing, group, and squadron) remain responsible for the security, safety, and handling of nuclear weapons and materials regardless of where they may be in the generation or employment process. For additional discussion on surety, see chapter 4.

SUMMARY

C2 involves the ability to gather information, make decisions, and communicate orders to forces in the field. Command relationships should be clear and understood by all personnel in the chain of command. Procedures must be in place to allow for accurate processing and authentication of orders. Communication systems must allow commanders to exercise control under a wide range of conditions. Timely and accurate information allows decision makers to examine the situation and develop options. C2 is an essential component in the effective employment and deterrence value of nuclear weapons.

CHAPTER THREE

PLANNING AND SUPPORT CONSIDERATIONS

> *In many ways, the challenge to sustain the excellence of our nuclear forces is greater today than ever. The operational demands of the Global War on Terrorism coupled with the costs of fielding modern forces across the Department of Defense continue to challenge our nuclear enterprise. The need to appropriately establish priorities and balance resources has never been more difficult.*
>
> **—Air Force Blue Ribbon Review of Nuclear Weapons Policies and Procedures, February 2008**

As with all military operations, nuclear operations may be carried out against an enemy's military, political, economic, and information targets. The goal is to achieve national objectives by neutralizing or destroying the enemy's war-making capabilities and will to fight.

Plans for nuclear operations are prepared by USSTRATCOM and the geographic combatant commands, in accordance with guidance provided by the President, SecDef, and the CJCS. These plans respond to threat assessments, targeting directives, and policy requirements. Accurate and timely intelligence is critical to planning nuclear operations.

PLANS

Nuclear operations can either be preplanned against specific targets using planned routing or adaptively planned against emerging targets. Preplanning provides the opportunity to conduct detailed planning and analysis against targets without the time pressures normally associated with a crisis action scenario. Preplanned options maintain centralized control while minimizing response time. Plans provide a variety of targeting options, which allow national leadership the flexibility to achieve objectives. As circumstances change during a conflict, adaptive planning allows leadership to retarget and strike emerging, mobile, or previously unknown targets. Quick reaction by nuclear forces can prevent enemy leadership from using resources to its advantage.

Planning for theater-level nuclear operations should be integrated into the CCDR's operational plans. This will maximize the desired effects, identify and prioritize intelligence, planning, and force requirements, and ensure proper levels of coordination and support necessary for successful mission operations. USSTRATCOM is tasked by the Joint Strategic Capabilities Plan to provide specific support to geographic CCDRs for their nuclear planning. Liaison teams are assigned to work with the joint force commander and the components in the development of nuclear options.

Planners may integrate nuclear options with conventional or non-kinetic operations to enhance effectiveness and minimize collateral effects. In some scenarios, the delivery of a single or a few nuclear weapons may require conventional support in the form of air superiority, defense suppression, air refueling, and post-strike assessment. In other scenarios, theater nuclear weapons may be integrated within a larger strike that also includes delivery of conventional ordnance. In other scenarios, CONUS-based bombers or submarine-launched cruise or ballistic missiles may support theater operations. All scenarios require careful planning to ensure integration of all capabilities, beyond simple deconfliction of weapons effects.

Given the fluid nature of the modern security environment, the need for strategic intelligence may be greater than ever. For planning to be effective, emerging threats should be identified long before they pose a significant danger to US interests. A strong link between intelligence and planning allows for the recognition of threats in advance and enables the US to take steps to deter or prevent their emergence and defend against them when required. Successful planning requires more than just an understanding of today's environment; it demands a forward-thinking paradigm that is proactive, rather than reactive, in nature.

TIMING AND DECONFLICTION

Nuclear employment is closely coordinated to combine targeting, mutual support, and defense, as well as national strategies and objectives. The options contained therein provide sufficient detail to ensure mutual support and defense suppression. Of particular concern is the timing and deconfliction of weapons. Fratricide, or the destruction of one weapon by another, will reduce the effectiveness of the nuclear strike. Planners coordinate between different weapons to ensure they do not conflict. Air Force planners and USSTRATCOM liaison teams in a theater of operations must also ensure that weapons are deconflicted before being employed.

Another issue of particular concern is the risk of friendly casualties. Planners should fully understand the effects of the weapons, applicable meteorological data, and location of US or allied forces. The impact to the US Government will be far greater than anticipated if it should turn out that US or allied forces are killed by their own nuclear weapons.

AIR, SPACE, AND CYBERSPACE SUPERIORITY

As with most Air Force operations, nuclear operations rely on and complement actions conducted across all domains. Despite the unique nature of nuclear weapons, operations must still be integrated to achieve assigned objectives. As articulated in Air Force doctrine, success in air, land, sea, space, and cyberspace operations depends upon air, space, and cyberspace superiority. They provide freedom to attack as well as freedom from attack. This is as true for nuclear missions as it is for any other form of attack.

Air, space, and cyberspace superiority strongly enhance nuclear operations by protecting manned systems and space assets. They deny enemy access to space for purposes of surveilling and targeting US forces, as well as inhibiting enemy nuclear C2. In addition, control of these domains allows US forces to be warned of and assess ballistic missile attacks, target enemy locations, exercise positive control of nuclear systems, conduct damage assessment, and plan follow-on operations. For more discussion on the various aspects of superiority, see AFDD 1, *Air Force Basic Doctrine, Organization, and Command*; AFDD 3-01, *Counterair*; AFDD 3-14, *Space Operations*; AFDD 3-13, *Information Operations*; and AFDD 3-12, *Cyberspace Operations*.

COMBAT SUPPORT

Effective support is critical for Air Force nuclear forces to be successful. Nuclear support structures must be organized, sized, and maintained to support all likely nuclear operations. Nuclear support includes such things as scheduled maintenance and support of current operations; generating bombers and ICBMs for nuclear alert in a crisis; deployment into a theater of operations, as required; and dispersal and reconstitution actions (before and after hostilities). Support structures should operate effectively throughout the range of military operations, including nuclear operations. When considering the possibility of nuclear options, planners must review the support issues involved and ensure all support requirements are met before moving weapons to new locations.

Security is an important concept in day-to-day support, as well as in dispersal and deployment operations. Weapons are particularly vulnerable when in transit or deployed under ad hoc field conditions, so appropriate measures must be taken to protect them. Planners and commanders should consider, among other things, the current threat level and local community concerns.

Maintenance for nuclear weapons and their delivery systems requires specially-trained personnel. The decision to deploy or disperse nuclear weapons also requires the deployment or mobilization of maintenance personnel, who typically require their own facilities separate from conventional munitions. Planners need to incorporate such unique support requirements when planning for nuclear operations away from an established infrastructure.

Because nuclear systems and facilities are lucrative targets, air base personnel may encounter CBRN weapons effects. US forces should be capable of responding to and executing operations in a CBRN environment with minimal degradation of force effectiveness. Implementing the principles of CBRN defense—avoidance, protection, and decontamination— will help preserve the fighting capability of the forces. AFDD 3-40, *Counter-Chemical, Biological, Radiological, and Nuclear Operations*, JP 3-11,

Operations in Chemical, Biological, Radiological, and Nuclear (CBRN) Environments, and JP 3-41, *Chemical, Biological, Radiological, Nuclear, and High-Yield Explosives Consequence Management*, provide additional guidance.

SUMMARY

Nuclear operations require careful planning. Plans should be developed in advance to provide alternatives to the President and should include preplanned options, while also maintaining the flexibility to adapt to changing situations. Just as USSTRATCOM operations plans have been created for strategic scenarios, theater commanders will develop appropriate nuclear contingencies in their campaign plans. These plans should take into account deconfliction with other weapons and means to avoid friendly casualties. In making the decision to move nuclear weapons, the commander must understand the significant logistical, security, and support concerns, such as airlift and maintenance facilities, which will require resources that might be used elsewhere. Commanders must be aware of the requirements of nuclear operations long before such weapons are ever employed.

CHAPTER FOUR

SURETY

> *As the United States reduced its nuclear stockpile following the end of the Cold War, emphasis on nuclear weapons declined and the forces assigned to operate, maintain, and support the nuclear capability reduced accordingly, especially in flying units. The ongoing challenge to the USAF is how to achieve a focused, dedicated nuclear capability with a smaller, but equally professional work force.*
>
> **—Air Force Blue Ribbon Review of Nuclear Weapons Policies and Procedures, February 2008**

"The goal of the Air Force Nuclear Weapons Surety Program is to incorporate maximum nuclear surety, consistent with operational requirements, from weapon system development to retirement from the inventory" (AFI 91-101, *Air Force Nuclear Weapons Surety Program*). This program applies to materiel, personnel, and procedures that contribute to the safety, security, and control of nuclear weapons, thus assuring no nuclear accidents, incidents, loss, or unauthorized or accidental use. The Air Force continues to pursue safer, more securable and more reliable nuclear weapons consistent with operational requirements.

Adversaries and allies should be highly confident of the Air Force's ability to secure nuclear weapons from accidents, theft, loss, and accidental or unauthorized use. This day-to-day commitment to precise and reliable nuclear operations is the cornerstone to the credibility of our nuclear deterrence mission.

Whether working with CONUS-based nuclear forces or conducting theater nuclear operations, commanders must ensure the safety, security, and reliability of their weapons and associated components. While the appropriate infrastructure already exists at CONUS bases with nuclear forces, geographic CCDRs should consider the additional needs incurred if they are going to have nuclear weapons deployed into their area of responsibility.

Two events that occurred in 2006 and 2007 alerted senior Department of Defense (DOD) officials to unacceptable practices in the handling of nuclear weapons and nuclear weapons-related materiel within the U.S Air Force. One incident was the unauthorized weapons transfer from Minot Air Force Base (AFB) in North Dakota to Barksdale AFB in Louisiana in August 2007, which was due to a breakdown in procedures in the accounting, issuing, loading, and verification processes.

The other incident involved the misshipment of four forward-section assemblies used on the Minuteman III intercontinental ballistic missile (ICBM). The assemblies are sensitive missile components and, as such, require special handling. Owing to errors and omissions in inventory control and packaging, on two separate occasions in October and November 2006, assemblies were sent to Taiwan. These shipments were intended to fulfill a foreign military sales order for helicopter batteries. Because of subsequent deficiencies in supply chain management, the components were not properly recovered until March 2008.

Despite the decreased inventory of nuclear weapons, there has never been a stated or implied willingness on the part of national leaders to permit, allow, or tolerate a lessening of the "zero-defects" standard regarding the safety, security, and reliability of U.S. nuclear forces or weapons. Yet, the investigations that followed each of these incidents revealed a serious erosion of expertise and discipline related to the nuclear weapons enterprise within the Air Force.

-- Report of the Secretary of Defense Task Force on DOD Nuclear Weapons Management, Phase I, September 2008

SAFETY

All individuals involved with nuclear weapons are responsible for the safety of those devices. Because of the destructive potential of these weapons, and the possibility that their unauthorized or accidental use might lead to war, safety is paramount. Per Department of Defense (DOD) Directive 3150.2, *Department of Defense Nuclear Weapons System Safety Program*, four specific nuclear surety standards must be met.

○ There shall be positive measures to prevent nuclear weapons involved in accidents or incidents, or jettisoned weapons, from producing a nuclear yield.

○ There shall be positive measures to prevent deliberate prearming, arming, launching, or releasing of nuclear weapons, except upon execution of emergency war orders or when directed by competent authority.

✪ There shall be positive measures to prevent inadvertent prearming, arming, launching, or releasing of nuclear weapons in all normal and credible abnormal environments.

✪ There shall be positive measures to ensure adequate security of nuclear weapons.

These measures include inherent warhead design features that prevent accidental or unauthorized nuclear yields, delivery platform design features, and operational procedures that prevent accidental or unauthorized use. The positive measures may take the form of mechanical systems, such as permissive action links that do not allow the arming or firing of a weapon until an authorized code has been entered. They may also involve personnel monitoring systems, such as the Personnel Reliability Program (PRP) or the Two-Person Concept. Commanders are responsible for ensuring that appropriate systems are in place, as described by appropriate Air Force policies. To track the implementation of these positive measures, the Air Force certifies its nuclear weapons systems. The Air Force's Nuclear Certification Program includes safety design, weapon compatibility, personnel reliability, technical guidance, specific job qualifications, inspections, and Weapons System Safety Rules (WSSR). Refer to AFI 63-125, *Nuclear Certification Program*, and AFI 91-101, *Air Force Nuclear Weapons Surety Program*, for more specific guidance.

Weapon System Safety Rules

WSSR ensure that nuclear weapons are not detonated, intentionally or otherwise, unless authorized. Safety rules apply even in wartime. While commanders may deviate from a specific rule in an emergency, they may not expend a nuclear weapon until an authentic execution order has been received. This has led to the so-called "usability paradox." Nuclear weapons must be "usable enough" so an enemy is convinced they may be rapidly employed in the event of an attack. They must not be so "usable," however, as to allow for the unauthorized use due to individual action or mechanical error.

WSSR are implemented through a combination of mechanical means, security procedures, flying rules, and personnel programs. Different weapon systems will have different rules based on their capabilities. Storage and movement of weapons must also be consistent with WSSR. Commanders and operators must follow applicable Air Force policies for their weapon system and must ensure that non-US personnel adhere to applicable Air Force and multinational requirements. One key component of WSSR is that, while preventing the unauthorized use of nuclear weapons, they allow for timely employment when ordered. To this end, all personnel involved in the command, control, and support of nuclear weapons must be familiar with WSSR for their system.

SECURITY

Nuclear weapons and their components must not be allowed to become vulnerable to loss, theft, sabotage, damage, or unauthorized use. Nuclear units must ensure measures are in place to provide the greatest possible deterrent against hostile acts. Should this fail, security should ensure detection, interception, and defeat of the hostile force before it is able to seize, damage, or destroy a nuclear weapon, delivery system, or critical components.

Commanders are accountable for the safety, training, security, and maintenance of nuclear weapons and delivery systems, and reliability of personnel at all times. Whether on a logistics movement or during an airlift mission, commanders should limit the exposure of nuclear weapons outside dedicated protection facilities consistent with operational requirements. Commanders must ensure that nuclear weapons and nuclear delivery systems are maintained according to approved procedures. Commanders are responsible for considering the additional needs incurred if nuclear capabilities are deployed into their operational area.

A security infrastructure exists at bases that routinely handle nuclear weapons. However, weapons and their delivery systems may be moved to other bases to enhance survivability or may be deployed into a theater. Commanders at such locations must ensure appropriate storage facilities are established and proper security measures are in place. The storage of nuclear weapons on a base not only requires a secure location and additional security personnel, but also impacts other areas such as driving routes, local flying area restrictions, aircraft parking areas, the use of host-nation or contract personnel, and other aspects of day-to-day operations. Note, too, that weapons are most vulnerable in transit or when deployed for use, so special care must be taken at those times. Commanders and, in fact, all individuals have a responsibility for force protection, and the security of nuclear weapons is a key component of that concept. Air Force policies which outline security requirements must be understood by all affected personnel.

Airmen should neither confirm nor deny the presence or absence of nuclear weapons at any general or specific location. This US policy applies even if a particular location may reasonably be assumed to contain nuclear weapons, such as a missile launch facility or a bomber base. The goal of this policy is "to deny militarily useful information to potential or actual enemies, to enhance the effectiveness of nuclear deterrence, and contribute to the security of nuclear weapons, especially against the threats of sabotage and terrorism." (DOD Directive 5230.16, *Nuclear Accident and Incident Public Affairs Guidance*)

RELIABILITY

The Air Force employs positive measures to ensure the reliability of its nuclear weapons systems and personnel to accomplish the mission. Reliability is also a product of the system's safety features, including safety design, weapon compatibility, personnel reliability, technical guidance, specific job qualifications, and nuclear technical inspections. Independent inspections and staff assistance visits are also an integral part of maintaining nuclear surety.

Weapon System Reliability

Through sustainment, testing, and modernization, the Air Force ensures the reliability of nuclear weapon systems. The Air Force engages the Department of Energy's National Nuclear Security Administration and other government agencies to ensure nuclear warheads and related interfaces continue to meet Air Force warfighting requirements. The Air Force continues to provide essential leadership of interagency reliability groups to include test planning, interface requirements and performance, and warhead design reviews.

Individual Reliability

Commanders ensure that only trained, certified, and reliable people have access to nuclear weapons, delivery systems, and C2 systems. The PRP is used to initially qualify, certify, and then monitor personnel assigned to nuclear operations tasks throughout their assignment. The PRP ensures that only those persons whose behavior demonstrates integrity, reliability, trustworthiness, allegiance, and loyalty to the US shall be allowed to perform duties associated with nuclear weapons. The Air Force also employs techniques such as the Two-Person Concept in all nuclear operations to ensure compliance with established procedures. The Two-Person Concept requires the presence at all times of at least two authorized persons, each certified under the PRP, knowledgeable in the task to be performed, familiar with applicable safety and security requirements, and each capable of promptly detecting an incorrect act or improper procedure with respect to the task to be performed.

SUMMARY

The Air Force implements a stringent surety program to assure that nuclear weapons and their components do not become vulnerable to loss, theft, sabotage, damage, or unauthorized use. All individuals involved with nuclear weapons and nuclear weapon components are responsible for the safety and security of those devices at all times.

CHAPTER FIVE

TRAINING

> *It is a doctrine of war not to assume the enemy will not come, but rather to rely on one's readiness to meet him; not to presume that he will not attack, but rather to make one's self invincible.*
>
> **-- Sun Tzu, *The Art of War***

The credibility of the Air Force's nuclear program is founded in the skill of its combat crews and support personnel. Realistic training, high standards for technical competence, strong analytical skills, and personal reliability are key elements that shape its force. The importance of high-quality training cannot be overstated.

Training for Air Force members in nuclear operations is conducted by a variety of organizations. In most cases initial training is conducted within a consolidated system, while recurring training is performed by the individual unit. Initial and recurring training in both the functioning of the weapon system and wartime procedures are critical if the highest possible standards of performance are to be maintained. Commanders must also place similar emphasis on readiness and proficiency in consequence management, security, and disaster preparedness as they would on operational employment.

TYPES OF TRAINING

Some Air Force members find themselves working only in nuclear operations, while others must be prepared to transition from conventional to nuclear missions. In either case, training requirements are very strict due to the sensitive nature and destructive potential of nuclear weapons.

ICBM and aircraft crews require an understanding of both their weapon system and EAP. Extensive weapon system training allows crew members to perform day-to-day operations and respond to weapon system failures and emergencies. Thorough EAP training ensures crews can provide a timely response to orders from the President and helps them understand how the degraded environment of a nuclear exchange will differ from day-to-day operations. In the time-sensitive environment expected in nuclear operations, crew members often will not have the time to read through manuals and policy documents, so in-depth EAP training is critical.

LEVELS OF TRAINING

For Air Force members in the nuclear arena, training is a continuous process. Initial and recurring training must provide nuclear personnel with the highest possible degree of skill and the most current information on weapon systems and procedures.

Initial training is focused on the knowledge level of learning. It introduces the crew member to nuclear operations and develops basic skills necessary to be a contributing member. Initial training focuses on what to do rather than why it is done. It enables the student to perform the mission. Once crew members can perform the essential tasks required of them, they are ready to expand their abilities through recurring training.

Recurring training allows crew members to move on to the application level of learning. They learn more about how their systems work, enabling them to resolve problems when the system does not function as it is supposed to. It is also a means of sharpening basic skills and educating personnel about changes in policies and procedures. Finally, it prepares individuals for increased responsibility for training others, leading forces, and planning operations.

EXERCISES AND WARGAMES

Exercises and wargames are effective means of maintaining and honing the skills of commanders, planners, and combat forces. Exercises involve moving actual forces, while wargames, which are generally for the benefit of commanders and staffs, simulate the movement of forces. They may be conducted at the base, unit, or command level or be Air Force-wide.

Exercises are vital to employing a credible deterrent force. Although nuclear forces train regularly and provide a deterrent effect through their day-to-day operations, recurring exercises are an excellent opportunity to refine training actions and procedures. Realistic scenarios provide linkages to other organizations and pinpoint issues that may be otherwise undiscovered. To avoid isolated training within various units, exercises allow for the integration of

The Air Force nuclear capability is, in fact, a force-in-being that achieves its goals by not being employed in war. As John Milton once wisely observed, "They also serve who only stand and wait." But the long uneventful periods of successful deterrence can have a corrosive effect on vigilance, responsiveness, and currency in the absence of unflagging motivation by leaders and frequent nuclear exercises. There are two major, interrelated purposes for exercising nuclear forces: deterrence and proficiency. Exercises provide a visible demonstration of capability and proficiency in mission execution to motivate restraint by potential adversaries.

-- Report of the Secretary of Defense Task Force on DOD Nuclear Weapons Management, Phase I, September 2008

operations with C2 elements via battle staff functions. This integration is not possible without exercising the nuclear force and perfects our deterrent procedures.

While it is imperative for nuclear forces to practice during training scenarios, exercises and wargames also provide a measurable effect of deterrence. Public announcements of planned or ongoing exercises give an authentic view of our nuclear capability to current or potential adversaries. This provides verifiable evidence of our deterrent capabilities and projects our resolve to the rest of the world.

While exercises are useful, it is important to consider all the implications of conducting one. First, safety and nuclear surety are paramount, and great care must be taken anytime weapons or nuclear facilities are involved in an exercise. Second, distinctions between real-world activities and exercise activities must be explicit so there is no question as to whether actual or simulated actions should be performed. Those distinctions should be clear to others as well; training activities may appear provocative to an adversary and should be designed to avoid precipitating a conflict. Finally, large-scale exercises may not afford the opportunity to stop and start again, applying lessons along the way. This is one primary advantage of wargames involving small groups of people.

SUMMARY

High-quality training is essential for high-quality performance. Personnel working in nuclear operations must maintain the highest standards of competence, rather than simply meeting the minimum. Training in normal and emergency weapon system procedures, as well as in combat operations, prepares crew members to react quickly to orders and changing situations. Recurring training should build upon initial training to further develop capabilities within the crew force. Exercises and wargames are effective means of training forces and commanders, and the differences between the two allow for training that is tailored to the needs of the student.

At the very heart of warfare lies doctrine...

REFERENCES

Air Force

(Note: All AFDDs are available at https://wwwmil.maxwell.af.mil/au/lemay/.
All AFDDs, both draft and approved, are also available at the LeMay Center doctrine Community of Practice at:
 https://afkm.wpafb.af.mil/community/views/home.aspx?Filter=OO-OP-AF-44)

AFI 63-125, *Nuclear Certification Program*
AFI 91-101, *Air Force Nuclear Weapons Surety Program*

Joint

(Note: All JPs are available at https://jdeis.js.mil/jdeis/index.jsp)

JP 1, *Doctrine for the Armed Forces of the United States*
JP 1-02, *Department of Defense Dictionary of Military and Associated Terms*
JP 3-11, *Operations in Chemical, Biological, Radiological, and Nuclear (CBRN) Environments*
JP 3-41, *Chemical, Biological, Radiological, Nuclear, and High-Yield Explosives Consequence Management*
JP 3-60, *Joint Targeting*

Department of Defense

DOD Directive 3150.2, *DOD Nuclear Weapons System Safety Program*, 23 December 1996 (certified current as of 8 March 2004)
http://www.dtic.mil/whs/directives/corres/pdf/315002p.pdf

DOD Directive 5230.16, *Nuclear Accident and Incident Public Affairs (PA) Guidance*, 20 December 1993 (Certified Current as of November 21, 2003)
http://www.dtic.mil/whs/directives/corres/pdf/523016p.pdf

Other Publications

The National Security Strategy of the United States of America, May 2010.
http://www.whitehouse.gov/sites/default/files/rss_viewer/national_security_strategy.pdf

The National Defense Strategy of the United States of America, June 2008.
http://www.defenselink.mil/pubs/2008NationalDefenseStrategy.pdf

The National Military Strategy of the United States of America, February 2011.
http://www.jcs.mil//content/files/2011-02/020811084800_2011_NMS_-08_FEB_2011.pdf

National Military Strategy to Combat Weapons of Mass Destruction, 13 February 2006.
http://www.defenselink.mil/pdf/NMS-CWMD2006.pdf

Air Force Blue Ribbon Review of Nuclear Weapons Policies and Procedures, 8 February 2008. (FOUO)

Report of the Secretary of Defense Task Force on DOD Nuclear Weapons Management, Phase 1: The Air Force's Nuclear Mission, September 2008 ("Schlesinger Report")
http://www.defense.gov/pubs/Phase_I_Report_Sept_10.pdf

Report on the Unauthorized Movement of Nuclear Weapons, Defense Science Board Permanent Task Force on Nuclear Weapons Safety, February 2008
http://www.defense.gov/npr/docs/DSB%20TF%20on%20NWS%20Welch%20Feb%202008.pdf

"Reinvigorating the Air Force Nuclear Enterprise," Air Force Nuclear Task Force, 24 October 2008
http://www.af.mil/shared/media/document/AFD-081024-073.pdf

Chief of Staff of the Air Force (CSAF) Professional Reading Program

The CSAF's professional reading list, with links to book reviews, is available on the Air Force web site at: http://www.af.mil/information/csafreading/index.asp. The list is subject to revision. Readers are encouraged to check the Air Force web site (http://www.af.mil) for the most current information.

Suggested Readings

Gray, Colin S., *Nuclear Strategy and National Style* (Hamilton Press). 1986.

Kahan, Jerome A., *Nuclear Threats from Small States* (US Army War College Strategic Studies Institute) 1994.

Magyar, Dr. Karl P. (ed.), *Global Security Concerns: Anticipating the Twenty-First Century* (Air University Press) 1996.

Paulsen, Richard A., Major, USAF, *The Role of Nuclear Weapons in the Post-Cold War Era* (Air University Press) 1994.

Sagan, Scott D., *The Limits of Safety* (Princeton University Press) 1993.

Walker, Martin, *The Cold War: A History* (Henry Holt and Co.) 1993.

GLOSSARY

Abbreviations and Acronyms

ADCON	administrative control
AFDD	Air Force Doctrine Document
C2	command and control
CBRN	chemical, biological, radiological, and nuclear
CCDR	combatant commander
CJCS	Chairman of the Joint Chiefs of Staff
COMAFFOR	Commander, Air Force Forces
CONUS	continental United States
DOD	Department of Defense
EAP	emergency action procedures
EMP	electromagnetic pulse
ICBM	intercontinental ballistic missile
ISR	intelligence, surveillance, and reconnaissance
JP	joint publication
MAJCOM	major command
NATO	North Atlantic Treaty Organization
OPCON	operational control
PRP	Personnel Reliability Program
SecDef	Secretary of Defense
US	United States
TACON	tactical control
USSTRATCOM	United States Strategic Command
WMD	weapon(s) of mass destruction
WSSR	weapon system safety rules

Definitions

administrative control. Direction or exercise of authority over subordinate or other organizations in respect to administration and support, including organization of Service forces, control of resources and equipment, personnel management, unit logistics, individual and unit training, readiness, mobilization, demobilization, discipline, and other matters not included in the operational missions of the subordinate or other organizations. Also called **ADCON**. (JP 1)

air superiority. That degree of dominance in the air battle of one force over another that permits the conduct of operations by the former and its related land, sea, and air forces at a given time and place without prohibitive interference by the opposing force. (JP 3-30)

assessment. A continuous process that measures the overall effectiveness of employing joint force capabilities during military operations. It is also the determination of the progress toward accomplishing a task, creating a condition, or achieving an objective.... (JP 3-0)

command and control. The exercise of authority and direction by a properly designated commander over assigned and attached forces in the accomplishment of the mission. Command and control functions are performed through an arrangement of personnel, equipment, communications, facilities, and procedures employed by a commander in planning, directing, coordinating, and controlling forces and operations in the accomplishment of the mission. Also called **C2**. (JP 1)

cyberspace superiority. The operational advantage in, through, and from cyberspace to conduct operations at a given time and in a given domain without prohibitive interference. (AFDD 3-12)

deterrence. The prevention of action by the existence of a credible threat of unacceptable counteraction and/or belief that the cost of action outweighs the perceived benefits. (JP 3-0)

nuclear weapon. A complete assembly (i.e., implosion type, gun type, or thermonuclear type), in its intended ultimate configuration which, upon completion of the prescribed arming, fusing, and firing sequence, is capable of producing the intended nuclear reaction and release of energy. (JP 3-11)

nuclear weapons surety. Materiel, personnel, and procedures that contribute to the security, safety, and reliability of nuclear weapons and to the assurance that there will be no nuclear weapon accidents, incidents, unauthorized weapon detonations, or degradation in performance at the target. (JP 1-02)

operational control. Command authority that may be exercised by commanders at any echelon at or below the level of combatant command. Operational control is inherent in combatant command (command authority) and may be delegated within the command. Operational control is the authority to perform those functions of command over subordinate forces involving organizing and employing commands and forces, assigning tasks, designating objectives, and giving authoritative direction necessary to accomplish the mission. Operational control includes authoritative direction over all aspects of military operations and joint training necessary to accomplish missions assigned to the command. Operational control should be exercised through the commanders of subordinate organizations. Normally this authority is exercised through subordinate joint force commanders and Service and/or functional component commanders. Operational control normally provides full authority to organize commands and forces and to employ those forces as the commander in operational control considers necessary to accomplish assigned missions; it does not, in and of itself, include authoritative direction for logistics or matters of administration, discipline, internal organization, or unit training. Also called **OPCON.** (JP 1)

operational level of war. The level of war at which campaigns and major operations are planned, conducted, and sustained to accomplish strategic objectives within theaters or areas of operations. (JP 3-0)

space superiority. The degree of dominance in space of one force over another that permits the conduct of operations by the former and its related land, sea, air, space, and special operations forces at a given time and place without prohibitive interference by the opposing force. (JP 3-14)

strategic attack. Offensive action specifically selected to achieve national strategic objectives. These attacks seek to weaken the adversary's ability or will to engage in conflict, and may achieve strategic objectives without necessarily having to achieve operational objectives as a precondition. (AFDD 3-70)

tactical control. Command authority over assigned or attached forces or commands, or military capability or forces made available for tasking, that is limited to the detailed direction and control of movements or maneuvers within the operational area necessary to accomplish missions or tasks assigned. Tactical control is inherent in operational control. Tactical control may be delegated to, and exercised at any level at or below the level of combatant command. Tactical control provides sufficient authority for controlling and directing the application of force or tactical use of combat support assets within the assigned mission or task. Also called **TACON.** (JP 1)

www.ingramcontent.com/pod-product-compliance
Lightning Source LLC
Chambersburg PA
CBHW080630290526
45790CB00007B/3000